P[O]

HERCULANEUM
VESUVIUS

Editions KINA ITALIA

Distributed by GUARDASOLE S.r.l. – Phone: 081/5590329

Introduction

Pompeii, Herculaneum and Vesuvius: three places which symbolise tourism and culture in Campania; three places which are so well known as to need no introduction. They are viewed with different eyes: on the one hand the two towns, concealed for centuries under the dust of history and slowly uncovered to provide an invaluable insight into life in the 1st century of the Christian era, are mainly famous for their historical and archaeological interest; on the other hand, the world-famous volcano is of greater interest to nature and landscape lovers. Yet Pompeii, Herculaneum and Vesuvius share a common historical legacy which has always linked their names and their destinies: the eruption of 79 A.D. The originator of this legacy, namely the volcano, with its horrific violence, was the devastating cause of the disappearance of the two towns, the silent sentry watching over their buried remains and, in the last analysis, the deadly creator of their glory. Pompeii and Herculaneum now constitute two historical relics with no equal anywhere in the world; the insight they provide into past life is not limited, as in the case of many other archaeological sites, to the physical appearance of the town, its planning, architecture and art. Something living remains of these two towns, however paradoxical it may seem; something that visitor has no difficulty seeing, or rather perceiving, as he walks along the streets, passing by private homes and tradesmen's shops, reading on the walls the political slogans and advertisements of nearly 20 centuries ago, marvelling at the wealth of some patrician residences or discovering that even so long ago, families lived in rented out apartment buildings, and glimpsing, through the remains of the furnishings of a home, at least something of the domestic atmosphere which must have existed there so long ago. A visit to Pompeii and Herculaneum always gives the strong impression of a moment in time suddenly frozen, stopped short, which comes back to life today. This impression is received not only from the dramatic, tragic testimony provided by the plaster casts of the bodies of those who were unable to flee the violence of the catastrophe, but above all in the surviving objects: the walls, the cobblestones furrowed by the passage of cartwheels, and roads which still seem to ring with the everyday sounds of two living towns. Wondering what would have become of these two towns if they had not been so dramatically swallowed up by the eruption of Vesuvius is obviously pointless; the point is, however cruel it may seem, that Pompeii and Herculaneum would certainly not be what they are today if the volcano had not buried them in that long-ago summer of 79 A.D.

VESUVIUS

History

It is not difficult to imagine the kind of profound impression that the first adventurous navigators must have felt (probably Phoenicians and then Greeks) when at the dawn of history they found themselves facing such spectacular scenery provided by a natural bay, surrounded by breath-taking limestone crests on one side and gentler projections of tuff on the other, and dominated by the unmistakable contours of a volcanic formation, the source of unknown and surprising phenomena, replete with atmosphere and mystery. And indeed, that cone, Vesuvius' characteristic profile, set in the background of what would later become universally known as the Bay of Naples, became a loved and celebrated image even among the first, ancient inhabitants of what is one of the most attractive areas along the entire peninsular coast. Clear evidence that this was so has been found both in mural pictures and in the oldest literary documentation. The last to be formed among the volcanic oreography of the Campania region, its origin has been placed by the experts amid the telluric formations of some twelve thousand years ago. The Vesuvius complex has certainly been responsible for the most disastrous eruptions witnessed by, presumably, vulnerable and terrorised prehistoric and early historical man. Today, in the plain to the south-east of the parthenopean city, it is the only active volcano on the continent

Panoramic area of the Gran Cono

of Europe and certainly among the most famous and studied volcanos in the world. Yet in the classical period it probably did not provide any great reason for worry in a population settled at the limit of its slopes. It has now been geologically verified that it was then passing through a long period of tranquillity, at least starting from the 8th century B.C. In addition it seems quite certain that at that time the highest point was somewhere around 2000 meters (as against the 1270 metres today) and that its slopes were covered with luxuriant forests and, lower down, by various types of cultivated crops, especially vineyards. The characteristic and entirely unmistakable shape of the

A print of the eighteenth century which depicts the volcano as it appeared at the time of the Pompeii and Herculaneum excavations

Vesuvian mountain, which has become a symbol of the parthenopean city and its region, is derived from the seismic transformations which the previous volcanic structure of Monte Somma underwent in that far off period. Geological investigations have indeed verified an alternation of explosive and effusive phases in this older formation: the primitive Somma, so-called by the experts in its activity set in the quaternary era, and the old Somma, dating back instead to the period between the seventh and the fourth millennium B.C. experienced a sequence of eruptive periods with long intervening periods of calm. In particular, at the same time as the period of intense activity in the nearby volcanos in the flegrea area, Monte Somma gave no sign of

life and on the contrary, following a progressive telluric lowering, it was even submerged under the sea. On re-emerging it reawoke with alternating phases until the first millennium B.C. and enjoyed a long period of calm for a good eight centuries, until it was shaken in 79 A.D. by the terrifying eruption described in the celebrated letters of Pliny the Younger to Tacitus, in which among other things he gives an account of the tragic death of his uncle, Pliny the Elder, a notable naturalist and, fatally, an insatiable observer. It was precisely that catastrophic explosion in the year 79 A.D. which, according to geological reconstruction, gave rise to the present Vesuvian outline with its large cone inserted amidst the remains of an analogous preexisting and larger formation.

The eruptions

In the eruptive history of the Vesuvian system four great periods have been identified, each one further divided into various sub-periods, these too, separated by more or less long periods of calm. The volcanic structure known today as Vesuvius is made from the formation created in the course of the fourth period, that is the present one. The cause of the returning to activity of the volcano, occurring between pauses lasting many centuries, is attributed by the experts to an increase in the gaseous formations produced by the magma, following the mixing of original magmatic masses with sedimentary masses, within which there is the so-called "focus", that is, the centre of the burning material, located at a depth of approximately 5-6 kilometers. Concerning the prehistoric periods there are obviously only hypotheses, formulated on the basis of studies and their related deductions. It seems probable, however, according to these investigations, that in the pliocenic period Vesuvius had a cycle of submarine activity and only later did it emerge from the billows, so to speak, and switch to its surface activity. Certainly the eruptive displays in the prehistoric period must have been numerous and impressive: the evidence can be seen in the lavic formations still visible today on Monte Somma; the lava flows solidified on the lower slopes where, incidentally, Pompeii was built; and the numerous secondary cones which surround it (the most important of which is certainly that of Camaldoli). In all probability the last eruption in the period immediately preceding the present one, that is the third period, must have been explosive and almost certainly created that majestic crater which today forms the rim of Monte Somma. This was subsequently extended, in a later phase of demolition, due to land slides and meteoric erosion, during the rest phase enjoyed by the volcano during the Roman period. The experts date the start of the historical period of Vesuvius with the

Effusive phase: the gases produced by internal combustion are emitted both from the crater eruptive channel and from lateral openings

7

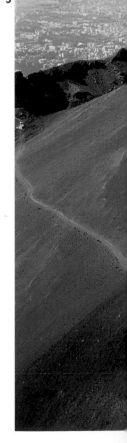

famous earthquake in 63 A.D. described by Seneca. This was probably a forewarning of the later and more terrible reawakening in 79 A.D. and we know that it had ruinous consequences for all the habitation centres at the foot of the mountain: from Naples to Herculaneum, to Pompeii and to Nocera. It was therefore this activity in 79 A.D. which constitutes the first historically documented eruption of the Vesuvius (described in the two famous letters by Pliny the Younger to the historian, Tacitus) sixteen years after the violent earthquake which had devastated the region. This time too, the phenomenon first announced its presence with several preliminary tremors, but when, finally, the violence of the gas and the incandescent material succeeded in once again opening the subterranean channel the eruption exploded skywards with appalling power. One whole side of the mountain was torn away for a length of two kilometers hurling out a fury of scoria, sparks,

boiling mud, poisonous gasses, lava, burning stones and ash. This then was the precise moment when, from that lesion, the so-called "Grande Cono" was created, that is the picturesque crater which has stubbornly continued, up to the last eruptive phenomenon in 1944, to send up its unmistakable plume of smoke, a sight for centuries associated with the image of Naples and its Bay. The eruption in 79 A.D. completely destroyed Pompeii, Herculaneum and Stabia, causing one of the most serious natural catastrophes in ancient history. The only naturalist to witness this frightening phenomenon was Pliny the Elder, who indeed finished as a victim

1) Arresting image of the snow covered crater
2-3) Panoramic views of the route leading to the crater

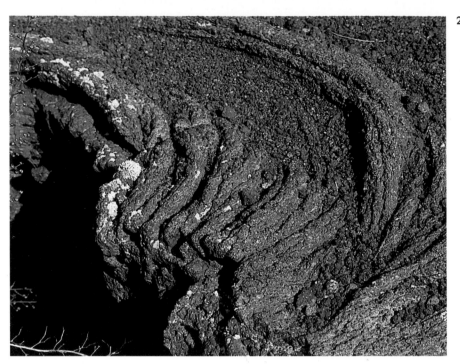

1) Detail of a typical "ropy" lava formation

2-3) Two moments during the climb to the crater

to his insatiable investigative curiosity. Farther away, and decidedly safer, his nephew, Pliny the Younger, at Capo Miseno, also observed what was happening and, later, around 106 A.D. he became its only official historian with what is the oldest written account of vulcanology - the two letters, that is, in which Pliny the Younger describes the details of the eruption with notes taken from those who had accompanied his uncle as well as everything he had himself seen. From these documents it is possible to extract not only precious information that helps to scientifically reconstruct the phenomenon, but it is also possible to get an idea of just how terrifying and frightening it must have been for both witnesses and victims. Equally significant for an understanding of the terrible desolation and the ruin left by the eruption is the famous epigram by

Martial, composed by the celebrated latin poet in 88 A.D.: *"This is Vesuvius, a short time ago green with vines; here the golden grape had pressed against the wet vats. This is the mountain that Bacchus loved beyond the Nisa hills, his homeland; on this mountain the Satyrs threaded their dances. This was the seat of Venus (Pompeii), more pleasing to her than Sparta; this place (Herculaneum) was famous through the name of Hercules. All lies buried by the flames and by a terrible conflagration! Not even the gods would have wished that such a thing had been done to them!"* And beyond the precise and detailed account by Pliny the Younger and the evocative verses by Martial, it is not difficult to grasp just how violent the eruption of 79 A.D. was when one considers that because of it the volcanic channel underwent a significant shift and the morphology of the contours

5
1-2-3-4) Some views of the route running from the Colle to the crater, across the Atrio del Cavallo

5) Detail of the path making it possible to descend into the interior of the crater

suffered those distinctive alterations which have given it its present day form. Early iconography, indeed, (a fresco discovered at Herculaneum and two more discovered at Pompeii) always depicts Vesuvius with a single summit and therefore before the split in the crater of Monte Somma. With regard to Vesuvian activity subsequent to the terrible episode of 79 A.D. there are only sporadic and flimsy reports; it seems that it can be characterised by what were for the most part explosive eruptions, with intervals of long periods of calm, sometimes lasting centuries.

The Vesuvius at night

POMPEII

History

Situated on the slopes of Vesuvius just a stone's throw from the sea, the ancient city probably developed from a small town which already existed in the 8th century B.C., based on an Osco-Campanian settlement founded in around the 6th century B.C., and developed rapidly as a result of its favourable location. Right from the time of its foundation, Pompeii was forced to defend itself against attempted domination by the more powerful populations of the area. In the 6th century, in order to avoid falling into the hands of the Etruscans, based in Capua, Pompeii entered into a treaty of alliance with the Cumaeans of Greek origin, who held sway throughout the Gulf of Naples.

However, the Etruscans still conquered Pompeii, which they dominated from 525 to 474 B.C., when they were defeated by the Greeks at the battle of Cumae. Released from Etruscan dominion, Pompeii again fell under Greek rule. The influence of these two great civilisations is clearly visible in the city's architecture (the examples of bucchero pottery with Etruscan inscriptions found in the city undoubtedly demonstrate Etruscan influence, while the "Doric temple" of the Triangular Forum is clearly of Greek derivation), as well as in the original urban structure and the primitive Pompeiian art. The city was next conquered by the Samnites, an Italic population from the interior of the region. In the following century, Roman troops began a campaign to conquer the Campania area, and by the end of the Samnite wars (343-290 B.C.) they dominated the entire region. Having routed the Samnites, as part of their strategy to subject the area's cities to the Capitoline power the Romans granted Pompeii the status of ally, guaranteeing it the privilege of retaining not only its language, but even its institutions. The flourishing years of the Samnite period, connoted by considerable urban expansion and the development of public and private architecture influenced by Italic art, were followed in the 2nd century by a period of even greater development, as a result of the Pax Romana and the improved communication and trade conditions created after the Roman conquest. Thus began a further expansion of the city, in which the imposing commemorative public buildings and the magnificent, elegant private buildings were inspired by the aesthetic tenets of Roman art. Comfort and prosperity failed to dispel Pompeii's desire for freedom and independence, and in 91 B.C. the city, together with other Italic towns, began the allies' war against Rome. The outcome of the revolt was unfavourable to Pompeii, which in 89 B.C. was first besieged and then occupied by the Roman militia, led by Silla. The defeat meant total loss of independence for Pompeii; it became a Roman municipality, and was governed until 80 B.C. by a quadrumvirate. It was then given the status of a Roman colony with the name Colonia Cornelia Veneria Pompeianorum, run by a local senate consisting of people friendly to Rome. In every sphere of life the city soon adopted Roman customs, which first supplemented and then gradually came to replace the customs of Italic origin which had dominated public and private life for centuries.

There was no abrupt, traumatic change; on the contrary, the gradual replacement, which was probably accepted readily by the majority of the population, coincided with the beginning of a new period of splendour for the city. Its economy and construction industry further expanded and developed, matched by an increase in its wealth and artistic sophistication. Only one episode disturbed the peace and prosperity of the city in the Imperial period: in 59 A.D., during the reign of Nero, a pitched battle was fought in the Pompeii amphitheatre between the inhabitants of Pompeii and those of Nocera. According to the historian Tacitus, it was a "horrific massacre", which began for trivial reasons relating to opinions about a group of gladiators (though what was really behind the riot was probably rivalry between the Italic populations which even Roman rule had not entirely suppressed). As a result, "the Senate banned this kind of meeting in the city for ten years". It was a natural calamity that violently aroused Pompeii from its golden torpor of peace and opulence. In 62 A.D. the city was seriously damaged by the earthquake which affected a large part of the Campania region. The Pompeiians reacted promptly to the catastrophe, almost immediately beginning the reconstruction work (especially in the private building sector) needed to restore the splendour and prosperity the city had enjoyed for centuries. But on 24th August of 79 A.D., the terrifying eruption of Vesuvius put an end to the fortunes of Pompeii for all time. Unlike Herculaneum and other towns in the area, which were buried under a river of mud, Pompeii (which by a tragic irony of fate was built on highly fertile land originating from a stream of lava that had erupted centuries earlier from the volcano) was hit by a gigantic cloud of poisonous gases, ash, lapilli and white-hot stones that buried monuments and human beings alike under a layer of debris as much as 7 metres deep.

Literally wiped out by the devastating fury of the volcano (which was described with tragic realism in a letter to Tacitus by Pliny the Younger, an eyewitness of the disaster), the city remained buried and forgotten by history for centuries. Traces of ancient buildings were discovered during the excavation of a canal in the early 17th century, but it occurred to no-one to associate them with the lost city. In the first half of the 18th century, following some accidental finds, the story of Pompeii was suddenly remembered, and in 1748 Carlo of Bourbon ordered the first systematic digs. The excavations, which continued in subsequent years with varying purposes and degrees of enthusiasm, were only conducted in accordance with strict scientific methods as from the late 19th century. Over 60 hectares of the area on which Pompeii must have stood at the time of the disaster have been excavated. Archaeological research is still continuing today, with the aim of preserving the remains already found and making new discoveries. The ash which suffocated the inhabitants of Pompeii in their desperate attempts to escape, or the equally vain attempt to take refuge in the innermost parts of the buildings (tragically demonstrated by the impressions of the bodies made in modern times), and caused the death of Pompeii has paradoxically preserved to the present day at least part of the life of this great city, protected by walls some 3 kilometres long; a city which was once prosperous, vital, bustling with pedestrians and traffic, and full of hotels, inns, post stages, shops of every kind, grandiose public buildings, temples and private homes, from the most modest to the most elegant and luxurious.

Painting

The essential element of decoration, namely painting, was of great importance in Pompeii, as can be seen on a visit to the ruins from the numerous works which still decorate the original rooms. From a certain period onwards, archaeologists wisely decided to leave the paintings in place instead of detaching them and moving them to the museum, thus enabling their elegance and taste to be more thoroughly appreciated. Pompeiian painting is divided into four styles covering different periods of time. The 1st style, situated chronologically between 150 and 80 B.C. and called the "encrustation" style, features decorative work which reflects the construction elements typical of public and private architecture: the walls are decorated with dados, pillars, columns and pediments in brightly-painted stucco.
This style of painting is of Greek/Hellenistic origin. The 2nd style, dating from between approximately 80 B.C. and the end of the Augustan period and called "architectural", also features numerous elements of architecture, but now with imaginative and sometimes daring perspective and multi-level effects which immediately recall the complex sets used in the theatre of the age to create the illusion of larger spaces, or even an opening to the exterior. Typical of this style are the splendid paintings of landscapes and gardens populated by animals and ornamented with fountains which "double" the real space, projecting it into a fascinating fantasy world. The 3rd style, known as the "Egyptian" style, dating from the death of Augustus (14 A.D.) to 62 A.D., when the city was damaged by the earthquake, was based much less on optical illusion. Here, the architectural structures lose their previous crucial role to become frames around the central pictorial scenes, which portrayed characters or episodes generally drawn from mythology. These were surrounded by other paintings, often miniatures, depicting human or mythological figures and landscapes decorated with patterns of Egyptian inspiration. Subsequently, until the eruption of 79 A.D., the 4th or "ornamental" style predominated in Pompeii. This style, characterised by the use of very bright colours, used various elements typical of the 2nd and 3rd styles. Fantasy, illusion and mythological motifs prevail, accompanied by very rich decoration which faithfully reflects the luxury and elegance of the homes in which it appears.

Sculpture

Another artistic expression of great importance in the decoration of the city's buildings was sculpture; works of great value and beauty came to light during the excavations. The materials mainly used were marble and bronze, together with less costly materials such as tuff, limestone and terracotta. Pompeiian statues are mainly small works, generally used to decorate the rooms of private homes. Pompeii's sculptors were strictly speaking craftsmen rather than artists; this distinction in no way detracts from the artistic value of the works found, but emphasises the mainly ornamental nature of the city's sculptures, produced to meet demand from the wealthier citizens who commissioned them. Some of Pompeii's small sculptures, generally inspired by Hellenistic sculptural art, reach heights of unexpected sophistication, like the famous bronze of the **dancing faun** that decorated the impluvium of the Faun House, outstanding for its elegant movement and soft limbs. The other two works of greatest value in this "minor" statuary are also bronzes: **the drunken young Satyr**, in which realism blends with a delicate artistic touch, and the dynamic group of the **Wild Boar attacked by Dogs**. In addition to these ornamental sculptures there are some larger works which must have had a religious or commemorative function. These include a number of copies of precious Greek originals such as **Apollo playing the Lyre**, possibly a copy of the original by Phidias, the bronze **Ephebe** found in Via dell'Abbondanza, the Attic original of which is dated by experts to the 5th century B.C., the superb marble copy of **Polyclitus' Doryphoros**, and the animated figures of **Apollo** and **Artemis** brandishing a lance, found in the Temple of Apollo. Portrait painting was quite popular in Roman Pompeii. Some outstanding examples are the realistic portrait of rich banker Lucius Cecilius, the portrait of theatre actor Caius Norbanus Soryx, permeated by a profound expressivity, and the statue in martial dress of the tribune Marcus Olconius Rufus, one of the most eminent citizens of Pompeii; despite its official air, this statue makes numerous concessions to sophisticated decoration.

Mosaics

Mosaic art constitutes a worthy accompaniment to pictorial art in Pompeii. In addition to wall paintings, many buildings, especially the most elegant and luxurious private homes, are decorated with mosaics which interpret the artistic canons that inspired painting at various periods in a highly original manner. For this reason, Pompeiian mosaic art is usually classified under different styles, roughly corresponding to various periods of history. A variety of materials were employed for the mosaics used to decorate either walls or floors, from simple fragments of humble terracotta to tesserae made of black and white stone or glass paste. The oldest mosaic floors in Pompeii date back to the period before the military occupation of the city by Silla's Roman troops.

The floors were spread with a layer of lime and covered with small fragments of terracotta or brick to form a very simple, sober decoration. In some cases, to enliven the effect, black or white pieces were inserted between the fragments of terracotta to form a geometrical pattern. In mosaics dating from the same period, small squares formed by coloured tesserae, portraying scenes inspired by nature, appear in a uniform floor covering. The first age of Roman Pompeii features mosaics with bold perspectives and optical illusions, as in the paintings of the same period. In these works, coloured pieces were cleverly positioned by the artists to create the shades of colour needed to bring the most original compositions to life. Later, artistic tastes returned to the geometrical simplicity typical of the early mosaics and the sober elegance of black and white decoration; the various geometrical and other patterns are framed by ornamental borders with various motifs. The last phase of Pompeiian mosaic work perfectly reflects the ornamental style which predominated in the art of the period. These colourful compositions, which featured magnificent decoration, mythological and fantasy figures, hunting and sailing scenes, plant and animal motifs, now decorated not only floors, but also the walls of houses and some public buildings (especially the baths), the fountains and nymphaea of the gardens, in a riot of vivacity and luxury.

Architecture

While the many and varied public buildings of Pompeii quite closely reflected the architectural canons found in other Italic cities, its private buildings offer a unique, extensive insight into the different construction types used over the centuries, from the pre-Samnite era to the Imperial period, culminating in the catastrophe of 79 A.D. The private homes and villas discovered in the urban and extra-urban area of Pompeii are important for two reasons: firstly because they demonstrate the different materials used and the various types and styles identifiable in the buildings, and secondly because they illustrate the everyday private and social life of its inhabitants, which can be deduced from the architectural structures of houses, shops, luxury villas and workshops.

In the construction field, the various historical periods of the city are characterised by the use of different materials for both public and private architecture. The oldest buildings, dating from the period prior to the Samnite conquest, were constructed with the materials available locally, especially sandstone and tuff; they generally have a very simple design, which mainly had to meet functional criteria. In the Italic period, construction materials of lava origin, also easily obtainable locally, were introduced in addition to tuff and sandstone. The designs used, though still sober, demonstrate greater attention to aesthetic aspects and denote a degree of Hellenistic influence. Both these types of private home – pre-Samnite and Italic – were built around a central atrium which was flanked at each end by rooms called *alae*, and surmounted by a four-pitched roof sloping towards the interior. A central opening in the roof (*compluvium*) provided lighting for the house and a supply of rainwater, collected in a tank below (*impluvium*), which communicated with a cistern. The other rooms (*cubicula*) were built around the courtyard, where the fireplace was located in ancient times, and the altar of the Lares was situated. At the end was the *tablinum*, originally a nuptial chamber and subsequently a reception room, from which access was obtained to the *hortus*, a garden of modest size. After the Roman conquest, buildings became more complex and diversified, and brick was used as well as local materials. Multiple atria were introduced, together with the peristyle, of mainly Greek derivation, which gave onto the various rooms, including new reception and rest rooms.

The *triclinium* (a dining room, also of Greek origin) became commonplace, and the small *hortus* often became a large cultivated garden, frequently ornamented by pools, fountains and sculptures. In the Imperial period, the taste for decoration and splendour led to the building of luxury dwellings and villas. The homes occupied by the less wealthy classes were far more modest, frequently built like modern terraced houses, and in some cases multi-storey.

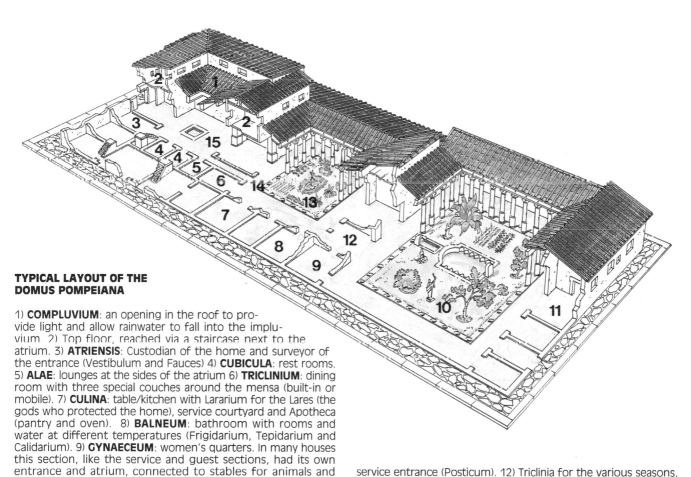

TYPICAL LAYOUT OF THE DOMUS POMPEIANA

1) **COMPLUVIUM**: an opening in the roof to provide light and allow rainwater to fall into the impluvium. 2) Top floor, reached via a staircase next to the atrium. 3) **ATRIENSIS**: Custodian of the home and surveyor of the entrance (Vestibulum and Fauces) 4) **CUBICULA**: rest rooms. 5) **ALAE**: lounges at the sides of the atrium 6) **TRICLINIUM**: dining room with three special couches around the mensa (built-in or mobile). 7) **CULINA**: table/kitchen with Lararium for the Lares (the gods who protected the home), service courtyard and Apotheca (pantry and oven). 8) **BALNEUM**: bathroom with rooms and water at different temperatures (Frigidarium, Tepidarium and Calidarium). 9) **GYNAECEUM**: women's quarters. In many houses this section, like the service and guest sections, had its own entrance and atrium, connected to stables for animals and coaches. 10) Second **PERISTYLUM** with large garden, almost always found in the larger homes. This garden was more likely than the former to be ornamented by a canal with springs and fish (Euripus), small temples, nymphaea with fountains and statues of divinities, pergolas (Vitea Tecta) and a triclinium for outdoor meals. 11) **OECUS** and **DIAETAE**: living rooms which overlooked the large garden. The house nearly always had a secondary or service entrance (Posticum). 12) Triclinia for the various seasons, or **OECI**. **EXEDRAE** and other living rooms mainly situated around the second and larger peristyle. 13) **VIRIDARIUM**: garden with fountains and statues, and sometimes the vegetable garden (Hortus). All around was the roofed colonnade (Peristylum). 14) **ANDRON**: corridor. 15) **IMPLUVIUM**: rainwater collection tank at the centre of the Atrium. At the edge of the tank was the sacred table, with the urn alongside (Cartibulum with Situla).

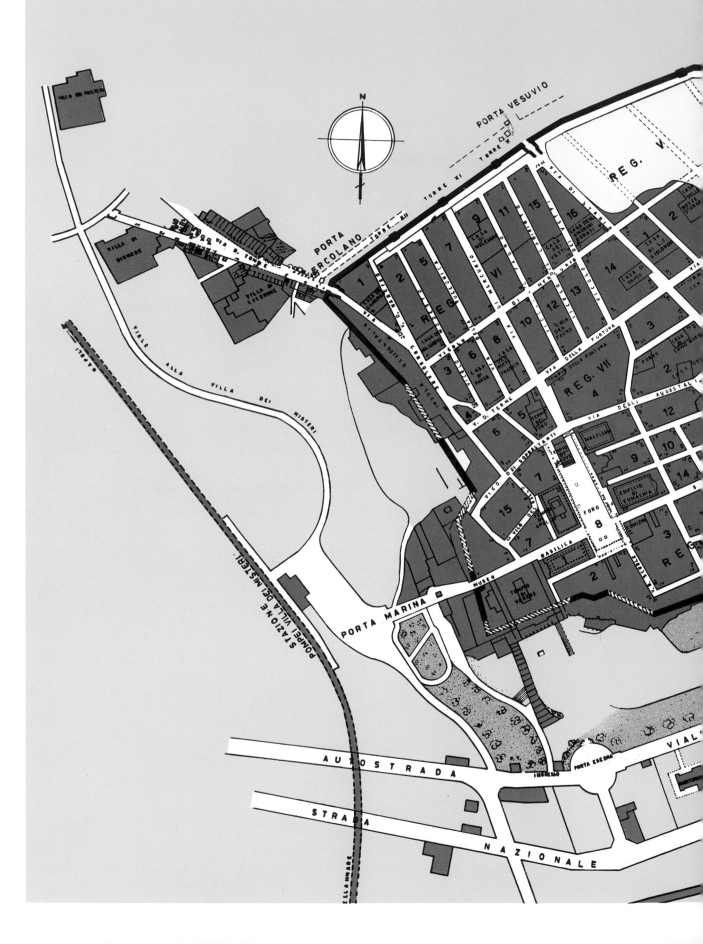

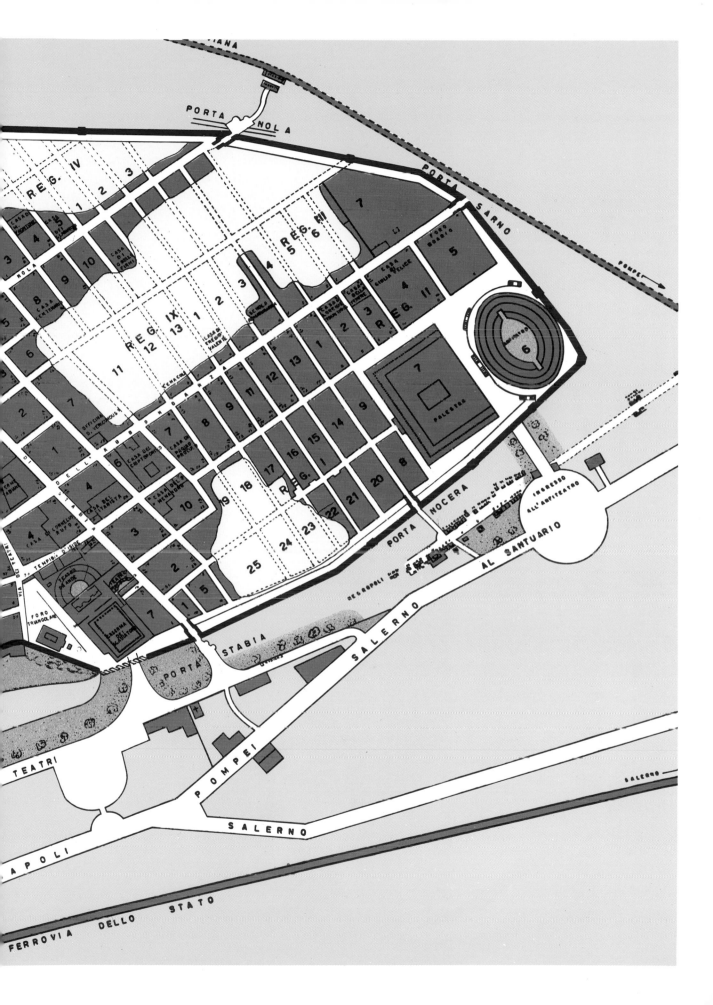

The Sea Gate

The fortifications of Pompeii are well preserved and we can see the entire perimeter and the structural characteristics of same. They were rebuilt many times from the 6th to the 1st century B.C. but from the appearances which were assumed in the Samnite period we can see a double curtain of square blocks reinforced by pillars and a support to which square cement towers were added in the last construction phase.

Only the uppermost parts are missing which must have been crowned with a patrolway and battlements. Close to the main roads were the gates which have deep passage-ways often divided into two sectors lengthwise. Owing to the preservation Sea Gate, Stabiana Gate, Nolana Gate and Ercolanense Gate give us an exact idea of their original appearance while other gates although interesting were found to be almost entirely destroyed (Vesuvius Gate and Sarno Gate).

In fact during the Roman period the walls and gates of Pompeii did not receive any particular care as they were no longer considered necessary during the climate of Roman peace. Many were actually demolished or incorporated into the houses and villas which were built on the town's edge. For the same reason, the damage caused by the earthquake to the gates was never repaired.

1

1) The Sea Gate

2) So called Imperial Villa - Detail of the Porch

The Suburban Villa

A suburban villa standing near the Sea Gate is sometimes mistakenly called the Imperial Villa. It was built making use of the defensive wall when this no longer had a defensive task and is constructed in terraces so as to appreciate the surrounding panorama.

The villa was partially destroyed in 62 A.D. but still shows evidence today of its complex architectural design. A long porch with paintings of the third style surround the garden and lead to the bedrooms, a triclinium hall and other rooms. The hall, preceded by a vestibule and bordered by passages is one of the largest covered rooms we know in Pompeian buildings and contains fine paintings showing scenes of Theseus and Icarus. The villa which has not been completely excavated must have been large and rich with other rooms, porches and a garden of which we only know a part.

The Forum

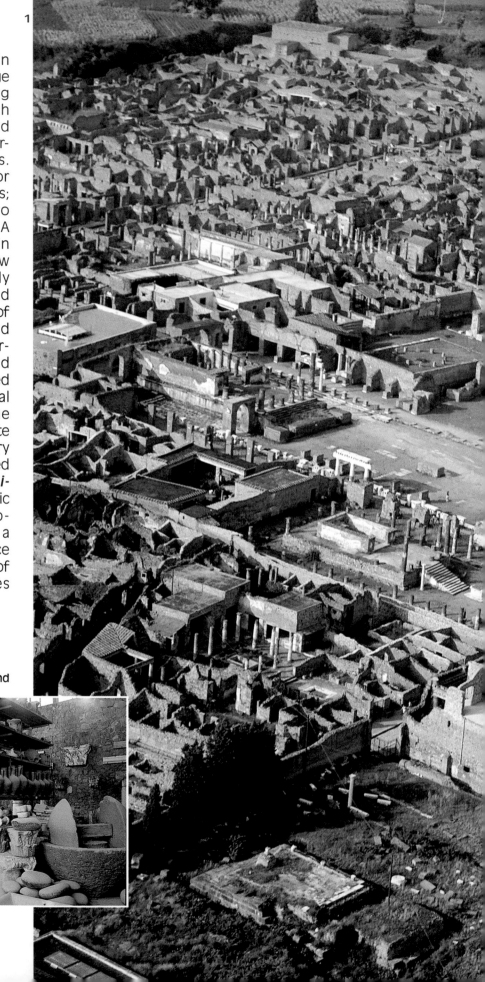

The centre of public life in Pompeii was the Forum, a large rectangular square stretching from north to south, with porches of different ages and styles on three sides and all surrounded by public buildings. Here the Pompeiians met for religious and political functions; to strike bargains or just to dally away their free time. A quick look at the buildings in the Forum shows us just how complex and animated daily life must have been. At the end of the square is the temple of Jupiter (father of gods and men) the most important worship place, here Juno and Minerva were also worshipped thus forming the traditional triad of Roman religion. The temple was built in the Samnite age during the second century B.C. and was later transformed by the Romans into the *Capitolium* of Pompeii. It is an Italic style temple, on a high podium the cell is preceded by a deep pronaos with a sacrifice altar in front. On each side of the temple are two arches

1) Aerial view of the excavations
2) Storehouse for archaeological funds
3) Section of Colonnade near Eumachia's Building
4) Section of Colonnade with the Temple of Jupiter in the background

3

4

erected in honour of members of the imperial family but we cannot identify them with any certainty. On the western side of the square are the public barns, the municipal treasury seat, the place where measures were controlled (*mensa ponderaria*) and finally the side of the sacred area where the temple of Apollo is situated. This is a place of worship going back at least to the 6th century B.C. but nowadays we see it as it appeared in the Samnite age with restorations made during the Roman period. To the south of the Forum are the public administration buildings, the seat of the duoviri, the most important magistrates in the town, that of master builders and the Senate house where the town Council assembled. Not far away stands the *Comitium*, an area used for elections. On the eastern side of the square is a building built

1) Reconstruction of the Civil Forum
2) Panoramic View
3) Temple of Fortuna Augusta
4) The Temple of Jupiter

at the expense of the priestess Eumachia – this was the seat of one of the most prosperous guilds in Pompeii, the *fullones'* who were manufacturers of woollen cloth. Then there is a small temple dedicated, it seems, to the emperor Vespasian and a small temple in honour of Public Lares. Next door is the *Macellum*, a large market with shops and also a shrine devoted to imperial worship. In the neighbourhood of the square are other public buildings, the temple of Fortuna Augusta, devoted to a religious cult characteristic of the Roman imperial world, as well as the Forum thermae and the Basilica.

1) A section of the Forum
2) The Temple of Vespasian
3) The Temple of Jupiter
4) View of Tiberius' Triumphal Arch

28

4

The Basilica

While in modern terms the Forum was the "city" of Pompeii, the Basilica was its "stock exchange" – the heart of its financial activities and of its civil and commercial litigation. The building which housed it, the most magnificent and solemn of all the public monuments in Pompeii, was constructed at the south-western corner of the Forum towards the end of the 2nd century B.C., as demonstrated by inscriptions in the Osco-Samnite language discovered on the site. The rectangular-plan Basilica covered a large area measuring 55 x 24 metres. The main entrance, preceded by an unroofed porticoed vestibule built above the level of the square, was unusually situated on a short side of the rectangle, just behind the portico of the Forum. There were two secondary entrances in the middle of the two longer sides. The interior was divided into a nave and two aisles: the large nave was surrounded by strong stuccoed pillars, while Ionic half-columns, originally supporting a second row of Corinthian half-columns, ran along the aisles. The shorter side opposite the entrance was occupied by the *tribunal*, raised on a dais, reserved for the Basilica judges. The building was abandoned after the earthquake of 62 A.D., in which it was badly damaged.

1) The Basilica
2) Panoramic view

The Temple of Apollo

Continuing north from the Basilica, along the west side of the Forum, the visitor comes to the Temple of Apollo, a solemn building which, as a whole, dates back to around the 2nd century B.C. In practice, as already mentioned, the cult of Apollo began in Pompeii at least as early as the 6th century B.C., as witnessed by numerous relics of the age found in the temple area; however, the building which now survives was only erected later. Over the centuries it underwent numerous major alterations, the last being those following the earthquake of 62 A.D., which badly damaged the building. The sacred area was originally surrounded by a majestic portico supported by 48 Ionic columns on which rested a Doric architrave; the latter in turn supported a second row of smaller columns. After the earthquake, stucco work on the columns of the lower row changed them into the Corinthian order, and the architrave received a new festoon decoration, while the upper columns were eliminated. At the centre of the area bounded by the portico is the heart of the temple, the cella, raised on a tall dais surrounded by Corinthian columns (six at the front and nine on the longer sides) and preceded by a staircase. This is where the statue of the god must have been kept; all that survives, however, is the base resting on a floor decorated with multicoloured patterns. At the foot of the staircase leading to the cella is the sacrificial altar, made of beautiful white travertine stone, which bears an inscription dating from the early years of Roman Pompeii. On the left is a white Ionic column, which once supported a sundial. The statues of divinities found inside the portico perhaps originally came from the nearby Temple of Venus. However, the bronze statues of Apollo and Artemis shooting arrows (transferred to the Naples Archaeological Museum and replaced by copies) definitely belong to the Temple of Apollo.

1) The excavations at Pompeii: The Temple of Apollo
2) Reconstruction of the Temple of Apollo
3) Temple of Apollo: detail

Roads

Pompeii gives us singular proof of the appearance of Roman roads and shows with what accuracy they were constructed. The roads are paved with a typical pavement of poligonal blocks of various shapes and sizes whilst a different method was used for paving large, open areas. The Triangular Forum and the area between the amphitheatre and the Gymnasium are not paved but in the Civil Forum square the pavement which was renewed more than once is made up of large square slabs. It is also noteworthy that here and there stone blocks were placed transversally to obstruct passage at that point. Characteristic also is the frequent presence of large cut stones crossing the road from one side to another – these allowed pedestrians to cross the road without getting wet when rainwater flooded the road – between each stone is a narrow space allowing the wheels of

1) Panoramic view of Via dei Teatri
2) Street with sewers
3) Street and fountain

1

2

34

3

the vehicles to pass. In fact Pompeii had a very limited sewerage system which was not sufficient to drain all the waste and rainwater. Evidence of the intense traffic in the town is given by the tracks, sometimes very deep, that the frequent passage of vehicles has cut into the road paving. The roads were usually bordered by pavements which varied in breadth and in type of paving. In front of the richest houses the paving was particularly well cared for, often with broken pottery mosaics. At many points on the edge of the pavement are holes where wooden poles were inserted to support curtains or tents put up in front of the houses or shops.

1-2) Typical structure of Pompeiian roads
3-4) Via della Abbondanza and fountain

The Triangular Forum

The large square which we usually call the triangular forum has gathered around it other monuments of Pompeii – for example the two theatres and the Samnite gymnasium and in the middle are the remains of a Doric temple. This temple goes back to the 6th century B.C. and shows the contact Pompeii had at this time with the Greek towns in Southern Italy and in particular Cumae. The temple was restored in the 4th-3rd century B.C. but later it was probably neglected and in the Roman age it had become a simple chapel. We do not know the gods to which it was dedicated but during the last period Hercules and Minerva were worshipped here. On the whole the Triangular Forum shows a noble architecture of the Samnite age with a high colonnaded vestibule and a Doric arcade surrounding the square.

1) Triangular Forum: Vestibule
2) Triangular Forum: detail

Theatres and Amphitheatre

Pompeii already had a building for theatrical performances in about the 5th century B.C. – it was a simple structure which made use of the natural land slope as the Greeks did and had a wooden stage. Over the centuries it was renewed many times, in the Samnite age tufa seats for the spectators were built and in the Roman age the flight of steps was enlarged and the stage rebuilt in stone with an articulated scenic front like the theatres in the larger towns in Italy and Asia Minor. Many of these adjustments were made thanks to the generosity of famous Pompeian citizens such as M. Antonio Primo, M. Olconio Rufo and M. Olconio Celere. We now see the theatre as it was after the last restoration in the Augustan age. The *cavea* with seats for the spectators is partially supported by a covered passage and to the sides are the *tribunalia* for the more important spectators. The orchestra pit which was no longer used for player's action was occupied by spectators as well. The stage is composed of a low stage where the actors recited and stately background with nooks, aediculas and three doors opening like the front of a palace, columns, tympanum and statues all helped to make the scene more attractive. The theatre could hold about 5000 spectators. Behind the stage was a square porched area where spectators stopped or sought shelter when the weather was bad. The Odeon stands near the theatre, it is a similar structure but much smaller and was used for artistic performances which attracted a smaller public, such as musical auditions, recitation of lines and miming and in fact could hold less than 1000 people. It was rebuilt about 80 B.C. thanks to the generosity of C.

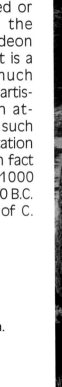

1) The Large Theatre. The Odeon. The Gymnasium
2) Large Theatre
3) Reconstruction of the Large Theatre

Quinzio Valgo and M. Porcio
and after this was never again
renewed. The flight of steps
has been very well preserved
and remains a noble example
of the late Hellenistic taste
flourishing in Pompeii and in
other areas during the last two
centuries B.C. The tuff *telamones* decorating the end of the
cavea are interesting examples of the sculpture of this
period. At the same time and
thanks once again to the generosity of C. Quinzio Valgo and
M. Porcio the amphitheatre
was built which could hold
20,000 spectators and this is
the oldest Roman amphitheatre which we know. The building
is partially enclosed by land but
it has no cellars and the entrances to the flight of steps have
outer steps. Here we do not
find the complicated structure
which characterizes the amphitheatres of the first imperial
Roman period. Near the amphitheatre there is a large
Gymnasium surrounded by
porches and a swimming pool
in the centre – here gladiators
trained as the many graffiti
testify.

1) View of the Large Gymnasium
2) Gladiator's helmet
3) The Amphitheatre

3

The Vettius House

This house belonged to a family of rich merchants and reflects the tenor of life of the wealthy class of Pompeii in the first century A.D. In the atrium are two safes and all around are rooms decorated with pictures of mythological subjects in the 4th Pompeian style. The house has no *tablinum* but the peristyle receives more attention. Here the garden has been reconstructed with elements furnished by the excavations and plants and fountains, so it appears as it must have looked originally. The rooms which open out here are decorated with fine murals and the tricliniar room is one of the most refined examples of Pompeian decoration – the walls have a red background split up by banded pillars and all around runs a frieze depicting cupids in everyday activities such as the selling of oil, biga racing, goldsmiths at work, gathering grapes, the wine market etc. The servants quarter with an upper storey is concentrated around a secondary atrium and there is also a flat with a porch reserved for the women.

1) The vettius House: peristyle (detail)
2) The Vettius House: lararium
3) A decoration with Cupids
4) The Vettius House: atrium

1) Decorations with Cupids (detail)
2) Apollo conquering the Python
3) Priapus weighing his phallus

3

1) Fresco
2) Cupid goldsmiths (detail)

The Brothel

This building, situated at the crossroads of Vicolo del Lupanare (Brothel Lane) and Vicolo del Balcone Pensile (Hanging Balcony Lane) is mainly interesting because it shows an aspect of social life which was quite important in Pompeii. The prosperous, lively, uninhibited city had numerous brothels, often on the upper floors of inns or houses, in which women who were nearly always of low class or from foreign countries like Greece or the Eastern provinces carried on their "trade". This brothel in particular, which had only recently been restored at the time of the eruption, must have had a considerable turnover, as demonstrated by the size of the building, with 10 rooms, five to each floor, and a balcony leading to the top floor. The wall paintings in each room, featuring highly explicit erotic scenes, probably indicated the services offered by the prostitutes. At the entrance to the brothel there was an obscene painting depicting Priapus with two phalluses, as if to make it quite clear what business was transacted in the building.

1) PAN AND THE HERMAPHRODITE
   From the House of the Dioscuri,
   Pompeii
2) EROTIC SCENE – House of the
   Centenarian, Pompeii
3) EROTIC SCENE – Wall painting from
   Pompeii

The Golden Cupid House

This small house, which belonged to a wealthy citizen of Pompeii, is mainly interesting for its sophisticated architecture and elegant pictorial decorations, often portraying mythological subjects, painted in the Imperial period. The atrium, flanked by painted bedrooms, leads to the unusual peristyle, which has one raised side decorated by a pediment supported by pillars to form a kind of stage; the masks hanging between the columns of the portico are also reminiscent of a theatre. On the north side of the portico is a bedroom with double alcove whose walls feature the elegant decoration after which the house is named: small glass discs to which pretty figures of cupids in gold leaf are appliquéd.

The Tragic Poet's House

This house, built in the Imperial period, had an unusual destiny. It definitely belonged to a wealthy shopkeeper, as demonstrated by the two shops flanking the vestibule and communicating with the house, but it has gone down in history as the Tragic Poet's House because the mosaic floor found in the *tablinum* portrays a theatrical rehearsal directed by a corego, who instructed the actors. Nevertheless, the house is usually remembered not so much for this elegant work as for the mosaic found on the vestibule floor (also of excellent manufacture but not as precious as the former), showing a dog grinding its teeth and the words "cave canem" (beware of the dog). The two-storey house

was decorated with elegant pictorial works inspired by Greek poetic cycles (including *Admetus and Alcestis* in the atrium, *Dido and Aeneas* in the triclinium, the *Sacrifice of Iphigenia* and the *Abduction of Chryseis*) or mythology (*Ariadne and Theseus*, *Venus and the Cupids*, *Marsyas and Olympus* in the triclinium), now preserved in the Naples Archaeological Museum. In architectural terms, the Tragic Poet's House is a combination of the typical Italic style, in which the atrium constitutes the core around which the main rooms are situated, and the style popular in the Imperial period, most evident in the rear of the

1) The House of the Golden Cupids: peristyle
2) The Tragic Poet's House: entrance mosaic (detail)
3) Marcus Lucretius Fronto's House

CAVE CANEM

house, with the peristyle, the elegant triclinium and the bedrooms ornamented by wall paintings.

The Lucretius Frontone's House

The main point of interest in M.L. Frontone's house is its wall decoration which is extremely well preserved and constitutes an excellent example of Pompeiian painting going back to the first imperial age. Other mythological paintings decorating the rooms are justly famous, for example Bacchus' triumphal retinue, Narcissus at the spring, Ariadne and Theseus and Orestes in Delphi. The house belonged to well-to-do people as we note from the decorations and the variety of rooms surrounding the atrium and in the rear around the garden is a summer triclinium. On the wall at the end of the garden is a large painting showing animals and trees in an African landscape.

3

The Ceius House

This house (the owner was L. Ceius Secundus) from its simple design evident especially in the four columned atrium and the decorations in the old Pompeiian style goes back to the pre-roman age but underwent radical changes in later times. In fact an upper storey was added which was reached by a stairway leaving from the atrium and divided by a gallery. This newer construction was carried out in a rustic style with a simple frame and is an interesting example of building transformation in private houses in Pompeii. In the atrium there was a wooden wardrobe, tracing of which has been obtained with the special method used in the excavations in Pompeii. At the end of the house is a small garden the walls of which are decorated with a large painting of a landscape with animals and trees.

The Menander House

This is one of the finest Pompeiian houses with noble architectural proportions and a detailed plan. Another branch of the family of Poppeae which we have already met in the Golden Cupid House, lived here. The façade facing on to the road is adorned with two tuff pillars with Corinthian capitals. The atrium is in the Tuscan style and the walls are decorated in the last Pompeiian style. In one corner is a little chapel for the worship of the domestic gods. Many rooms open out onto the atrium and one of them is decorated with little pictures of episodes from the "Iliad" – Laocoon, the Trojan horse and Cassandra. Gathered

1) The Ceius House: fresco

2) The Menander House: portrait of the poet Menander

around the peristyle which is at the rear are still more rooms. From one side we can see a large triclinium where the excavations have been carried out in layers showing the first construction phase of the house with wall decorations of the first style. In a small room nearby skeletons of the victims of the eruption have been found. Next come the servants quarters where the slaves lived and then the rustic lodgings and a small courtyard with a stable. At the end of the peristyle we can see paintings of theatrical subjects including a portrait of the poet Menander

and from this the house gets its name. From the other side of the peristyle it is possible to reach the bathroom which reproduces on a smaller scale and with refined pictorial decorations a typical thermal complex. The silver plate found in this house testifies to the wealth of the inhabitants.

The House of the Large Fountain

On the opposite side to the Anchor House is one of the characteristic Pompeiian workshops, a **fuller's shop**. This is a workshop with adjacent dwelling where woollen clothes were washed, and then dyed; the various operations were illustrated on a painted pillar, now in the Naples Archaeological Museum. Next to the dyers' was a mansion, the Large Fountain House, interesting for the ashlar facing of the façade. This house, like most of the more luxurious residences in Pompeii, had a small garden immediately beyond the atrium. On the back wall of the garden the owner built a grandiose nymphaeum, inside which he placed the work after which the house is named – a splendid mosaic-decorated fountain, among the most precious specimens of Pompeiian mosaic art. The backdrop to the basin is a niche surmounted by a small pediment entirely covered with coloured paste tesserae, which create surprising colour effects and a variety of ornamental patterns. An opening in the centre allows the water to gush out and fall back into the basin, cascading down the steps of a small staircase. The decoration of the fountain was completed by the two theatrical masks protruding at the sides, and the small bronze of a putto with a dolphin in the centre of the basin.

1) The House of the Large Fountain
2-3) Large Fountain House Mosaic
Nymphaeum

60

The House of Venus in the Shell

Here the construction is concentrated around the garden along which there is a two-sided porch. On the end wall is an airy, vivid painting with subjects relating to the garden – hedges with flowery bushes, marble basins with doves and even a Mars.

The large composition in the centre of the painting is Venus sailing the sea in a shell and escorted by two Cupids. Artistically speaking this is a modest work but must be appreciated for its decorative taste which harmonizes pleasantly with the garden and its flora.

The Orchard House

The vivid decoration which gives the name to this house (also called "the house of the floral cubicles") adorns the walls of two cubicles, one near the atrium and the other near the tablinum.

The paintings show figtrees, cherrytrees, strawberry and lemontrees which must have been rare in ancient Campania – birds and other animals give life to the picture which undoubtedly was inspired by the fertile Pompeiian countryside of that period. In the lower part of the painting trees, basins, enclosures give the idea of a garden and the fact that these subjects have been used for a painting inside the house and not in the garden or porch suggests that the house was inhabited by a rich fruitgrower who chose subjects close to his daily life. From Egyptian subjects found in the same cubicles it is also thought that worship of Dionysus-Osiris was practised here.

1) The House of Venus in the Shell
2-3) The Orchard House: Examples of the pictorial decorations after which the house is named

Lorelus Tiburtinus' House

This is a house of simple, harmonious proportions and a large part is given over to the green of the garden which stretches out at the back of the house and to the long loggia covered by a pergola. A stream with a small waterfall, fountains and statues of muses, animals and hermas adorned the whole setting. At the end of the loggia, in the open air, a triclinium is decorated with mythical subjects (*Pyramus and Thisbe* and *Narcissus*) and even if these paintings have no artistic value they are interesting as they were signed by the artist and man called Lucius.

The paintings in the hall were painted with more care – on two uninterrupted freizes are depicted the Trojan cycle and the labours of Hercules. In another small room is an elegant painting of many figures one of which is the figure of a priest of Isis and is thought to be the portrait of one of the inhabitants of the house.

Julia Felix's Villa

This house was built at the east end of the town and its several parts surround a large garden which is bordered on one side by a marble pillared porch and on the other by a pergola whilst in the centre is a large pool. Behind the porch are many rooms one of which is the triclinium and then the thermal quarter which we learn from the inscription was let for public use. Here we can recognise the characteristic elements – *frigidarium*, *tepidarium*, *calidarium* and a *laconi-*

3

4

cum for *sudationes*. Nearby is a block used for shops which had an upper storey and finally behind the villa is a large area with a kitchen garden and an orchard.

Diomedes' Villa

This villa opens out onto the Via dei Sepolcri with a small entrance which leads into the peristyle around which are situated the various parts of the villa.

To the east is the thermal quarter with a small porch and a pool for cold baths while to the north and south are a succession of rooms including the triclinium and an apse hall with three large windows. Opposite the entrance is the tablinium which leads on to the other part of the villa formed by a garden in a square area surrounded by porches supporting a balcony while in the centre of the garden is a pool and a summer triclinium.

This is a classic example of an urban villa plan in the imperial Roman age.

1) Lorelus Tiburtinus' House: the Garden
2) Julia Felix's Villa: portico and garden
3) Diomedes' Villa: peristyle
4) Diomedes' Villa: peristyle (detail)

1) A shop
2) The Baker's shop

Mills and Ovens

The shops and workshops in Pompeii offer us a valuable insight into the daily life of the Pompeiians and help to clarify what the contemporary writers wrote. Not only daily life with its vivid human aspects but also social and economic life with all its fascinating problems and multiform aspects.

The shops and workshops set in rows along the roads of the town occupy the ground floor rooms which have often only been transformed into shops during the last years of Pompeii when the merchants fluorished and the rich families began to decline. Often we can see that a mezzanine wooden floor had been constructed to

provide an abode for the seller (we still see this practice in our southern towns) and signs often remain of a small wooden porch which overlooked the road. On the outer wall of the shops we can note painted signs which drew passer-by's attention to what was sold in that particular shop or signs depicting divinities who it was hoped would help and protect the shop. Inside the shops and workshops we can gather from the furniture and equipment as well as from painted or graphite inscriptions what was sold there. At the entrance to the shops a long stone bench covered with marble or painted plaster was used to exhibit the goods – bulging amphoras on the counter held corn, oil and

wine and sometimes residues of the contents have been found during the excavations. A product found in the well-sealed amphoras is the *garum*, a kind of fish sauce and we can read the name of the sauce and the manufacturer of the sauce on the amphoras.

From all this evidence we can find out the agricultural production of the area, the goods imported and the diet of the Pompeiians. We must not forget the many *tabernae*, really public-houses and the *thermopolia* which rather looked like our bars – these were places where people met for a drink and a chat. One of these establishments was managed not by a landlord but by girls who seemed to have been activists

during the last Pompeiian elections. The bakeries have also proved to be very interesting – we can see the mill stones with which they produced the flour and nearby the table where the dough was kneaded and at the end of the room the oven. Pieces of carbonized bread have been found during the excavations and also an inscription testifying to the goodness of Pompeiian bread.

Obviously all the most important activities are recognizable in the shops – bread was sold either at the bakery where it was produced or in special baker's shops, there were fruiterers one of whom was a certain **Felix**, vegetable sellers, shoemakers, washerwomen and dyers, carpenters and blacksmiths and pastry cooks who, judging from the cake forms found must have been very skillful. To complete the picture we have the brothel giving us an interesting insight into the morals and the **hospitium** a modest inn organization for people who came from a distant place.

1) **Mill and Oven**
2) **A shop: detail**

The Forum Baths

Uncovered in 1824, a year after excavations began in the area of the civil Forum, the Forum Baths stand at the crossroads between Via delle Terme (Bath Street) and Via del Foro (Forum Street), behind the Temple of Jupiter. Their construction dates back to the early years of the Roman colonisation, around 80 B.C. The location and the building techniques used proved ideal on the occasion of the earthquake which damaged the city in 62 A.D.: compared with the other bath houses, the Forum Baths were not seriously damaged on the whole. They were rapidly repaired, as demonstrated by the fact that they were the only ones in operation anywhere in Pompeii at the time of the eruption. The baths, which also had a gymnasium, were divided into two sections, male and female (of less interest). Both sections had a changing room (*apodyterium*) and rooms for cold baths (*frigidarium*), lukewarm baths (*tepidarium*) and hot baths (*calidarium*). There were three entrances to the men's section: a corridor led from the Via delle Terme entrance to the changing room, with its vaulted ceiling, on which little trace of the original stucco decoration remains. The walls contained no recesses for clothes, which were probably placed in cupboards. From the *apodyterium*, an opening in the rear wall led directly to the cold bathroom, the walls of which were decorated with stucco friezes and pictorial representations. Bathers had to return through the changing room to reach the tepidarium, an attractive room whose ceiling is ornamented by stucco panels with various subjects. Along the walls are a series of recesses framed at the sides by terracotta Atlases supporting an elegant ornamental freeze with entwining plant motifs. At the centre of the room is the large bronze brazier which heated it, decorated with the insignia of the donor, Marcus Nigidius Vaccula, who also donated the three nearby bronze seats. We next come to the *calidarium*, ingeniously constructed so that warm air could circulate to heat the entire room. The large room with its stuccoed roof terminates at the end wall with an apse, at the centre of which is the *labrum* (the marble cold water bath destined for ablutions). The hot-water swimming pool was situated on the opposite side.

1) Apsidal calidarium
2) Forum Baths: Calidarium
3) Forum Baths: Tepidarium

Via dei Sepolcri

The principal roads connecting Pompeii with neighbouring towns were bordered, as was the classic custom, not only by villas and country houses but also by sepulchral areas, the necropolis. Side by side with poor graves are several rich sepulchral monuments which belonged to personages who held an important place in the history or public life of the town as well as to the most influential Pompeian families. Styles vary, some reflect Greek-Hellenistic funeral architecture while others follow the Roman Italic tradition and yet others reflect particular tastes and requirements.

1-2) Views of Via dei Sepolcri
3-4) Examples of Tomb Architecture

Often the points of greater distinction from the artistic point of view are found in the sepulchral enclosure which is surrounded by a low wall and included a small open area for burials in the earth and a columbarium room where the urns for ashes were kept. Two extraurban roads outside Pompeii possess the majority of these monuments, they are Via dei Sepolcri leading from the Herculaneum Gate and Via Nucerina but others have also been found outside Stabia Gate, Vesuvius Gate and places more distant from the town. Along Via dei Sepolcri we can see: the *Istacidis Mausoleum* – a circular temple set on a high podium and adorned with statues only one of which survives today, then there is the Tomb of Garlands one of the most ancient with its fine relief decoration, *M. Umbricio Scauro's Sepulchre* showing scenes from gladiator games in his honour, *C. Munazio Fausto* and his wife *Nevoleia Tyche's* sepulchre including a marble altar on which are sculpted a funeral ceremony and a ship lowering the sails – an important example of sculpture of the last years of Pompeii. Here also is the sepulchre of the Ceius family adorned with statues. No less interesting are the sepulchres found along Via Nucerina; the

1-2) Examples of Tomb Architecture
3) Via dei Sepolcri and Herculaneum
 Gate

74

Cuspis sepulchre with a columbarium room on top of which stands a circular monument, this same circular monument is found inside the funeral enclosure of the *Veia Barchilla's Sepulchre*. There is the funeral area belonging to the *Flavia family* who were freedmen with aediculas showing their dead's portraits and a square temple sepulchre which has statues of the dead in sitting positions, also the large exedra sepulchre of the priestess *Eumachia*, *M. Ottavio* and his relatives' monument formed by a four colonnaded temple with the dead's statues, the *Stronnis' Sepulchre* like a podium with crouched lions executed in the Hellenistic style and *Vesonis'* aedicula monument again with statues of their dead. All these funeral monuments usually have inscriptions telling us the names and rank of the personages buried there and in this way we can see the activity they carried out in Pompeii, follow episodes in their life, identify their house, the public works they performed and finally the place where they are buried.

Organic substances were not preserved over the centuries as those objects made from inorganic materials – slowly they disintegrated leaving an empty space – during the excavations when an empty space was noticed plaster casts were made to obtain the shape of what was in the empty space before it disintegrated. In this way casts have been made of the corpses of victims of the eruption, of trees, wooden objects, doors, cartwheels, furniture, etc. Here in the Pompeian antiquarium are kept many of these plaster casts – important relics of what otherwise would have been lost.

1) Tombs outside the Nocera Gate
2-3) Imprints of corpses found in a garden

Pages 78/79: Aerial view of the excavations

The Villa of Mysteries

This is perhaps the most famous and most highly admired house in Pompeii because it is the finest and most complete example of a large suburban villa and also because of its various rooms decorated with artistically superior paintings especially in the triclinium hall which contains the famous frieze which gives the villa its name.

The excavation of this villa which began in 1909-10 is not yet complete but it is thought that the small part still buried can add little to what we already know.

The first plan of the villa goes back to the second century B.C. but was later enlarged and rebuilt as a luxury house and its golden moment came during the Augustan Age when it became part of the imperial state property.

However after the earthquake it was reduced to a rustic villa and its last owners belonged to the Istacidi family. It is a large four-sided building built on a slope so that it rests partially on the ground and partially on a covered porch.

The entrance, not completely excavated leads onto a road of which we know only a small part and which was perhaps linked to Via dei Sepolcri.

To the sides of the entrance are the servants quarters with equipment for making pasta,

Large Painting Room

also an oven, the kitchens, wine pantry and a wine press. From the entrance passing through a small atrium we reach the peristyle where the true nucleus of this house begins, with rooms and halls for different uses and a group of thermal rooms.

Here is the large atrium, the tablinium and an apse veran-dah with a view of the sea. To the sides are still more rooms, cubicles, the triclinium with the famous large freize and porches dividing different groups of rooms. Passing through the verandah to visit the villa we note that this part of the buildings has hanging gardens and is supported by the aforementioned covered porch. The painted wall deco-rations have unequalled inter-est and reflect the different periods of the building life and the various uses it was put to. The decorations of the 3rd and 4th styles are less inter-esting but the tablinium is noteworthy with its black walls and Egyptian type symbols – however the most valuable are the paintings of the second style which were spared the changes the villa underwent during the last period.

A cubicle with figures linked to the myth and worship of Dionysus is decorated in the same style and this cubicle is used as an anteroom for the triclinium hall.

1) Large Painting Room: flagellated Woman and Naked Bacchante
2) Large Painting Room: reading of the Ritual and Girl offering Sacrifice

The large freize in this hall is of the second style and is the most complete example of a special type which we seldom see in the paintings of this period – here in fact is a continuous representation which occupies all the walls in the rooms with natural size figures. This freize was perhaps executed towards the middle of the first century B.C. by a local artist who drew inspiration from the works of Greek painters or was influenced by that style of painting and its classical rules. Scholars cannot agree to the paintings' meaning as it does not deal with an easily identifiable subject – it is composed of different scenes one after the other which deal with different stages of a rite about which we have no information.

It is believed that the painting is related to the mistery worship which existed together in the Greek-Roman world with the state religion but which was known only by a few selected men.

Many people believe that the freize deals with the various phases of the initiation of a bride to dionysiac mysteries – mysteries which were found in Campania in the Roman age. Thus we see in the various scenes both human and divine figures. The reason why the freize was painted here can be explained by the fact that the ladyowner was an initiator and minister of this cult.

The freize begins on the north wall near a small door – in the first scene a boy is reading the sacred ritual under the guidance of a noble lady while a woman in a mantle listens. The next scene depicts the sacrifice and offering with a pastoral group including Silenus playing the lyre. The wall at the end of the hall is dominated by two divinities to whom the rites are relative,

Dionysus and Ariadne, then to one side Silenian satyrs are intent on some mysterious deed whilst on the other side a woman reveals the symbol of fertility whilst a winged

Large Painting Room: the Terrified Woman

figure is in the act of striking with a *flagellum*. On another wall a whipped woman seeks refuge in her friends lap whilst nearby a naked Bacchante dances seized by orgiastic excitement. Lastly the bride dresses and the rite ends showing her sitting and mantled – now the initiated and mystic bride of the god.

Large Painting Room: the Sacrifice and Silenus playing his pipe

Herculaneum

Historical introduction

Herculaneum, founded by Hercules according to mythological tradition, actually did have Greek origins, as demonstrated by the few remaining traces of the most ancient city walls and the layout of the town, with cardines and decumani built at right angles. The Greeks of Neapolis and Cumae ruled Herculaneum as from the 6th century B.C., while in the 5th century the Samnites gained control, and the town remained under their domination for centuries.

Between the 2nd and 1st centuries B.C., Herculaneum took part in the allies' war against Rome, but in 89 B.C. it was conquered and transformed into a *municipium*. After the conquest it developed in demographic, political and urban terms. Its economy was not based on commerce and crafts; Herculaneum was a high-class resort with many patrician residences and few buildings destined for business activities, where life must have jogged on at a fairly relaxed pace.

In 63 A.D. the town was hit by the earthquake which devastated all of Campania. It had not yet recovered from that catastrophe when, on 24th August in the year 79 A.D., it was engulfed by a huge river of boiling mud and debris produced by the terrifying eruption of Vesuvius, which totally inundated it. The population probably had time to attempt an escape towards the sea, but they were forced back to the shore by a violent tidal wave, as witnessed by the human remains and remains of boats recently found along the coast.

When the eruption ended, Herculaneum was covered with a thick layer of mud (at some points over 10 metres deep); abandoned by its inhabitants, the town was never rebuilt, and only later did the town of Resina grow up at the edges of and partly on the area where Herculaneum once stood.

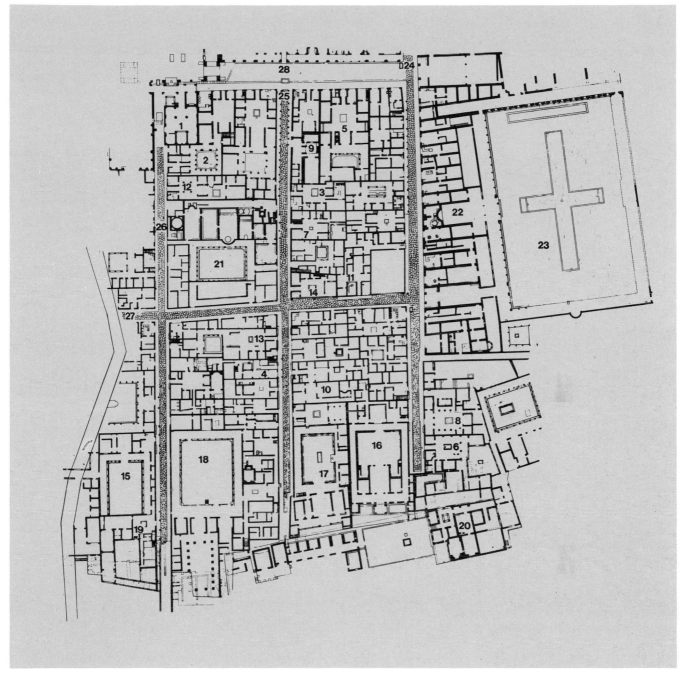

HERCULANEUM
Map of the excavations

Pages. 90/91: The Great Gymnasium

A brief history of the excavations

The very mud that sealed its fate has preserved the town to the present day. As it dried and solidified, it turned into a kind of thick, compact blanket which adhered to every structure and household article, thus protecting everything which escaped the river of mud and debris, and preserving (among other things) the upper floors of the buildings. Although numerous masonry structures were damaged by the shock wave, entire rooms have been brought to light practically intact. The layer of mud also preserved wood, a material which normally soon deteriorates unless suitably protected. The first discovery of remains of the ancient city was as recent as 1709, when the Austrian Prince d'Elboeuf discovered part of the Theatre by chance. Further research, conducted as from 1738 in accordance with the tunnel and shaft system, brought to light among other things the "Villa of Papyr", situated near the town, which is celebrated for its collection of sculptures and a library consisting of around 2000 papyrus scrolls. The excavations were closed in 1766; they only recommenced in 1828, this time using the more modern method of open-air excavation, and continued until 1855. In 1869 work began again, but the results were very disappointing, and excavation was interrupted in 1875. Amedeo Maiuri recommenced the research with scientific rigour in 1927, and it has continued until the present day.

Aerial view of the excavations

Visitor's itinerary

Access to the excavations is obtained from the entrance on Corso Ercolano. After leaving the ticket office, follow the viaduct which offers a view of the archaeological area, showing the town crossed by five cardines and three decumani and divided into "insulae" (blocks), then walk down to the garden of the Hotel House, between the 3rd and 4th Cardo, where the visit begins. To the left of the 3rd Cardo is the **Argus House**, a patrician residence with a portico that enclosed the garden on three sides. In addition to this first peristyle, there was a second, leading to the triclinium decorated by a fresco (now lost) portraying "Io watched by Argus". On the opposite side of the road, the **Hotel House** occupies

1) Deer House
2) 3rd Cardo
3) House of the Mosaic Atrium

a large part of the insula it belongs to. Originally believed to be a hotel (hence its name), it was later identified as a private patrician house. Continuing along the 3rd Cardo we come to the **Skeleton House**, so called because a human skeleton was found there. The building, which consists of three separate constructions, has a roofed atrium and two nymphaea, built as light shafts to illuminate the various rooms. Another interesting aspect is the drawing room, with its unusual apsidal ceiling and multi-coloured floor. The small courtyard to which it leads has a wall decoration portraying a garden. Turning right at the crossroads of the 3rd Cardo and the Lower Decumanus and right again at the crossroads of the latter with the 4th Cardo, we come to the **House of the Wooden Partition**, the outer façade of which remains intact as far as the second floor. On

1) Decumanus Maximum: cross of the 5th Cardo
2) View from above of the Decumanus Maximum
3) Decumanus Maximum: shops

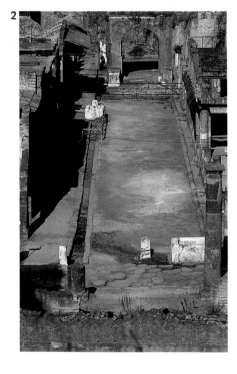

96

1) Argus House

2) 4th Cardo

the right of the large atrium, which has a compluvium roof and marble impluvium, is a bedroom with mosaic floor and a table supported by a statue of Attis. The lounge leading off the atrium was once separated from the hall by a three-leafed folding wooden door. Behind the lounge is a porticoed garden overlooked by the main room of the house. Next comes the *Grid House* (so called after the technique used to build the walls), an interesting example of a working-class house consisting of two separate dwellings rented by different families. After passing the *House of the Bronze Hermas*, whose tablinum is decorated by a bronze bust of the owner, we come to the *House of the Mosaic Atrium* on the opposite side of the street. Formed by two buildings, it is named after the checkerboard mosaic decorating the atrium floor. From the hall, through a windowed porti-

1) House of the Mosaic Atrium
2) House of the Wooden Partition
3) Skeleton House: mortuary
4) House of the Mosaic Atrium: detail
5-6) House of the Mosaic Atrium: floor
7) House of the Mosaic Atrium: the torment of Dircis

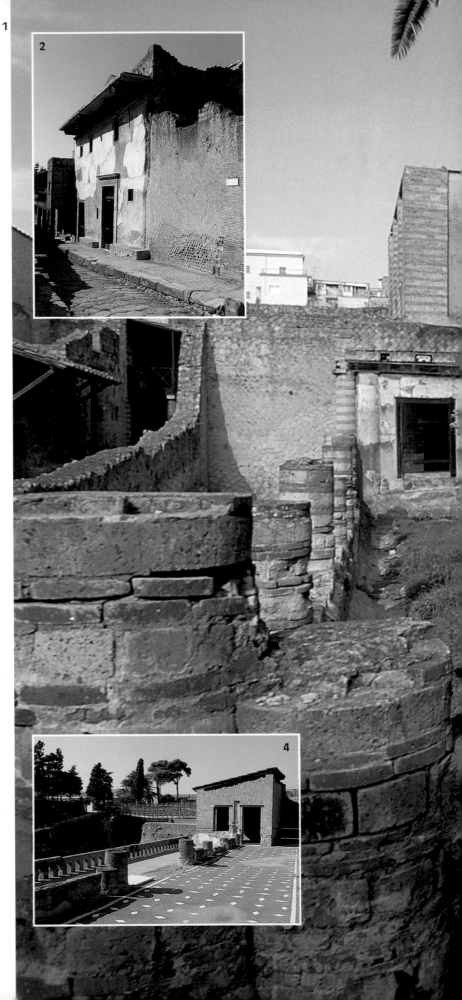

co (remnants of whose wooden framework are visible), we reach the garden, overlooked by bedrooms and an exedra embellished with mythological decorations. The other wing of the house is occupied by a series of small rooms with elegant decorations built around a large triclinium with opus sectile floor; the room overlooks a covered loggia which gives onto an open terrace below, overlooking the sea. Walking back along the 4th Cardo, immediately after the crossroads with the Lower Decumanus, we come

rooms, which give onto a roofed vestibule, suggests that the house is a reconstruction of part of the nearby Samnite House carried out during the Imperial age. After passing the **Fountain of Neptune** at the corner of the Lower Decumanus and the 5th Cardo and, further along, the largest shop found in Herculaneum and the **Fabric House** (where pieces of fabric were found), we come to the **Deer**

1) House of the Wooden Partition
2) Painting of the Samnite House
3) View of the Tuscanic Atrium in the Samnite House
4) House of the Great Portal

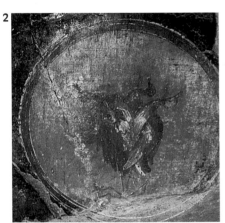

to what is called the **Samnite House** because it has numerous characteristics typical of the Samnite architecture of the 2nd century B.C. The ground floor of the house consists of a hall decorated with embossed coloured blocks of fake marble, an atrium with a large marble impluvium and a gallery with Ionic columns at the upper level, a cubiculum with a fresco portraying "The Rape of Europa", a large drawing room and a tablinum with an elegantly decorated floor. Next door, on the Lower Decumanus, is the **House of the Great Portal**, with an entrance portal surrounded by half-columns with Corinthian capitals decorated by "Victories". The arrangement of the inner

House. Built between 41 and 68 A.D., this is one of the most elegant homes in Herculaneum. The extensive building consists of a large rectangle divided into two areas: the north area comprises the hall and other inhabited rooms, and the south area consists of terraces overlooking the sea and connected by a four-sided windowed portico. The roofed atrium, whose walls have an alternating black and white background, leads to the triclinium, with its elegant marble floor decoration. The sculptured group of "Deer attacked by Dogs" after which the house is named was found in this room. Next, we come to the cubiculum, with its red-painted walls and marble floor, followed by a room with vaulted ceiling decorated in the same way. After crossing the large inner garden, around which runs a four-sided windowed portico with mosaic floor and walls decorated with elegant frescoes depicting

1-4) The inner garden of the Deer House
2) Drunk Hercules
3) Deer attached by dogs

4

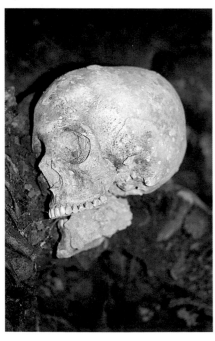

Human bones findings

"Cupids' Games", we enter the summer triclinium to the south, at the sides of which there are two small rooms decorated with precious marbles, followed by a loggia, also flanked by two rooms. Follow the ramp leading to the **Sea Gate** to enter the maritime district. Near the 4th Cardo there is an open space occupied by the marble base of a statue and a funeral altar, both dedicated to Proconsul Marcus Nonius Balbus. Next to this area are the square-plan **Suburban Baths**, the best preserved baths of antiquity (second half of the 1st century A.D.). The outer portal leads down to a vestibule, illuminated by a light shaft resting on four columns surmounted by twin arches. The vestibule gives onto the various rooms of the Baths, which have marble floors, seats and decorations, and in some cases, wooden door and window frames in an excellent state of preservation. The frigidarium leads to a room decorated with stucco reliefs portraying warriors. Next, we come to the tepidarium, the

1-2) Stucco reliefs of the Warriors
3) Altar built in celebration of Marcus Nonius Balbus
4) Pool in the Calidarium
5) Gem House

5

sudatorium and finally the calidarium. On leaving the Suburban Baths, follow the 5th Cardo to the **Gem House**, where a gem decorated with the portrait of a women was found. This is a single house divided into two areas: the most elegant part, at road level, comprises a magnificent atrium decorated with red and black wall paintings, a tablinum, a kitchen, a triclinium with mosaic floor in geometrical patterns, and a terrace overlooking the sea; the part at the lower level is more modest in appearance. Alongside is the *Telephus Relief House*, one of the most elegant and spacious in the district. This two-storey house has an atrium with columns supporting the rooms on the top floor. From the atrium, a corridor leads to the peristyle surrounding the garden, which has a basin with a blue background in the centre. Some rooms which retain part of the original pictorial and mosaic decoration open onto the adjacent terrace; the most attractive coloured marble house decoration which has survived from ancient times can be seen in one of them. A smaller room is decorated with a relief portraying the "Myth of Telephus". At the crossroads between the 5th Cardo and the lane which leads off to the right, we can visit the largest pistrinum (oven and mill) of the town, which contains two grindstones and various bakery tools. We next come to the *Gymnasium*, preceded by a large vestibule. The large unroofed rectangular area was surrounded on three sides by a Corinthian colonnade, and on the fourth side by a cryptoporticus which supported the spectators' gallery. The west wing features a

5th Cardo

magnificent apsidal room with the grey and white marble athletes' table in the centre, and two smaller rooms at the sides containing what remains of the original frescoes. At the centre is a long, cross-shaped swimming pool which was supplied with water by an elaborate bronze fountain portraying the Hydra in the middle. At the north end of

1) Thermopolium
2) Sundial
3-5) House of the Telephus relief: detail
4) Walls and columns with porch decorations on a red background, in the Telephus House

the Gymnasium is another vestibule with opus sectile floor,
which almost certainly housed a
public gymnasium. On the 5th
Cardo, opposite the apsidal
room of the Gymnasium, stands
the **Wooden Sacellus House**,
with its unusual temple-shaped
wooden sacellus used both as a
cupboard and for the worship
of the Lares. The next house we
come to is the **Corinthian
Atrium House**, preceded by a
small portico and a pavement
with elegant marble decorations. Inside there is an atrium
with six columns, three on
either side of the impluvium,
with its cross-shaped central
fountain. Also on the Decumanus Maximus stands the
Bicentenary House, where excavations concluded two centuries
after the beginning of research
in Herculaneum. Despite recon-
structions after the earthquake
of 63 A.D., the patrician style of
this residence is still evident on
the ground floor, which features
an elegant atrium, its floor
decorated with mosaic on a
black background and its walls

1-2-3) Detail of the Great Gymnasium
4) Great Gymnasium: bronze fountain
    depicting the Five Headed Hydra
5) A statue of the Imperial Family,
    located in the apse

1

2

3

4

5

decorated with paintings on a red background, and a tablinum with marble floor, walls decorated with panels and medallions portraying mythological subjects, and a frieze above depicting "Cupids". The lounge, in which a priceless sliding wooden gate was found, leads to the porticoed garden. A staircase leads to the top floor, occupied by rented rooms. The imprint of a cross-shaped emblem which, according to a controversial interpretation was the Cross of Christ, was found in one of them, demonstrating the spread of Christianity in Herculaneum before 79 A.D. The *Forum*, few traces of which survive, stood at the northern end of the Decumanus Maximus. On the left, near the crossroads with the 3rd Cardo, stands the portico of the Basilica, behind one of the two triumphal arches

which stood on the Decumanus. The square building to the south, with mythological scenes on the walls, must have housed the Curia, or the ceremonies of public worship of the Lares. The remains discovered on the opposite corner may be the *College of Augustals*. Turning into the 3rd Cardo from the Decumanus Maximus we come to the *Black Drawing Room House* and, almost opposite, the

1) Decumanus Maximum: detail of the façade of the Bicentenary House
2) House of the Black Atrium
3-4) Decorated walls of the Bicentenary House
5) Bicentenary House: Ariadne and Theseus (fresco).
6) Decumanus Maximum: fountain of Venus

Beautiful Courtyard House. The latter is a home of modest proportions with unusually distributed rooms, including a raised courtyard, with an elegant mosaic floor and a staircase leading to the gallery, decorated with pictorial motifs; the remains of furniture and charred wood carvings were found in the house. Walk down the Cardo to the two-storey *Neptune and Amphitrite Mosaic House*, which has a lovely summer triclinium and a nymphaeum decorated with coloured mosaics portraying "Neptune and Amphitrite" and "Hunting Scenes". The shop annexed to the house, in which the wooden structures and many of the furnishings are well preserved, is very interesting. Next comes the small *Charred Furniture House*, whose structure dates from the 2nd century B.C., which contains elegant mosaic and pictorial decorations

1) House of the Black Atrium: detail
2) House of the Beautiful Courtyard: detail
3-4) House of Neptune and Amphitrite: view of the inner court and the mosaic depicting Neptune and Amphitrite

dating from a later period (the age of Claudius). Some wooden furniture (a bed and a table) was found there, charred but in an excellent state of preservation. On the other side of the 4th Cardo, opposite the **Loom House** (a small weaver's shop where the remains of wooden material and parts of a loom were discovered), is the entrance to the **Baths**, built around

1) Central thermal baths: the gymnasium
2) Woman's Apodyterium
3-5) Man's Apodyterium
4) Calidarium (man's section): hollow apsis

120

4

5

10 B.C. and later redecorated. The complex has four entrances: one on the 3rd Cardo which gives access to the men's section, and three on the 4th Cardo, giving access to the gymnasium courtyard, the ladies' section and the room used to heat the water. The ladies' section is the smallest and least decorated, but has the best preserved structure. The men's section has the gymnasium area in the middle, which led directly to the large changing room. A passage on the left leads to the frigidarium, where the figures of fish decorating the vault of the dome must have been reflected in the water of the circular pool below. From here we return to the changing room, which leads onto the tepidarium, whose

1) House of the Double Atrium
2) House of the Double Atrium: painting in the 4th style, with still-life
3) College of the Augustals: cell

Pages 124/125: College of the Augustals: detail of the interior and commemorative inscription

3

AVGVSTO SACR
A A LVCII A FILII MEN
PROCVLVS ET IVLIANVS
P S
DEDICATIONE DECVRIONIBVS ET
AVGVSTALIBVS CENAM DEDERVNT

floor is decorated with a mosaic portraying a "Galloping Triton". The calidarium has a hot-water swimming pool on one side, and the dals of the labrum (tank for ablutions) on the other side, in an apse. Leave the Baths by the entrance on the 3rd Cardo and walk towards the Decumanus Maximus as far as the **Double Atrium House**, a two-storey residence with opus reticulatum façade, which has two atria. The first is tetrastyle, while the second, further inside the house, is the Tuscan type, and has an impluvium enclosed by a parapet. When the visit to the urban area of the excavations is over, it is possible to continue for a short stretch along Corso Ercolano to the area of the **Old Theatre**, built in the Augustan and post-Augustan periods.

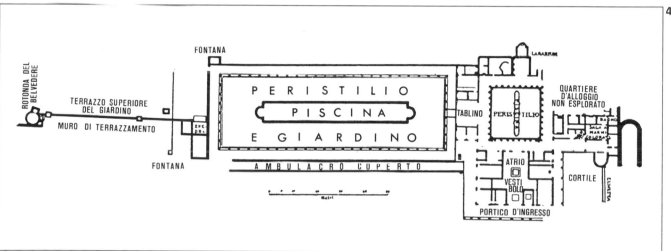

An equally interesting building in the neighbourhood of Herculaneum is the **Villa of Papyri.** Found during the 1738-1766 excavations, it contained priceless ancient material consisting of exquisite works of art and a huge library of papyrus scrolls, mainly dealing with philosophical subjects, discovered between 1762 and 1764.

The almost 2000 scrolls, found in a charred state caused by a natural chemico-physical process, are now in the Naples National Library. Access to the villa was gained through a magnificent entrance with colonnaded portico overlooking the sea, which led to the atrium, decorated with an **impluvium** ornamented with 11 statuettes, and then to the lounge and other rooms that gave on to a first peristyle, including the room destined to hold the library.

A second large peristyle (100 x 376 metres) with a large basin in the middle was built around the garden. Priceless marble and bronze sculptures, some of which are now on display at the Naples Archaeological Museum, were found in the gallery and the garden area.

From the garden, an avenue leads to a panoramic terrace decorated with an elegant inlaid marble floor.

1-2) College of the Augustals: frescos
1) The Herculanum Dancers
2) The floor plant of the Great Suburban Villa of the Papyri

INDEX